First Steps

A Few Initial Questions

CBMC is an international evangelical organization of Christian business and professional men whose primary purpose is to present Jesus Christ as Savior and Lord to other business and professional men and to train these men to carry out the Great Commission. (Matthew 28:18-20, Colossians 1:28-29)

CBMC is a nonprofit, nondenominational Christian ministry supported by gifts from people committed to reaching and discipling business and professional men for Jesus Christ.

Printed in the United States of America. ISBN 978-1-947457-09-6

CBMC, Inc.
P.O. Box 8009, Chattanooga, TN 37414-0009
www.cbmc.com, 800.566.2262

Is the Bible Credible?

According to Webster's Dictionary, one meaning of the word "bible" is "any book regarded as authoritative and official." For Christians, the Bible is God's authoritative and official revelation to man, composed of 66 books penned by 40 different authors over a span of 1500 years. Its authors came from every walk of life—kings, peasants, philosophers, fishermen, poets, statesmen, and scholars. It was written on at least three different continents in three different languages—Hebrew, Aramaic, and Greek—yet there is a thread of continuity from Genesis to Revelation, with the complete consistency of God's moral laws throughout. The Bible contains blatantly honest accounts of the lives of its main characters, exposing their strengths **and** their weaknesses.

In this lesson, we will examine and discuss why Christians believe the Bible to be the revealed Word of God.

Please note that all Scripture passages may be found at the end of each chapter.

1. **Read 2 Timothy 3:14-17.** When the apostle Paul wrote to young Timothy, what did he say the Holy Scriptures could do for him?

   _____

   _____

2. According to Paul, where did those scriptures originate?

   _____

   _____

3. Does Paul believe the Bible to be useful?

   _____

   In what ways or for what reason?

   _____

4. In the Old Testament alone, the authors claim to be writing or speaking God's words over 2600 times. The New Testament writer refers to these men in 2 Peter 1:19-21. According to these verses, where did their prophecy (prediction of the future) originate?

   _____

   _____

5. Whose words were they speaking? (v.21)

   _____

Prophecies About Jesus Christ

The New Testament was written to show us the character and teachings of Jesus Christ. The word "testament" means "covenant or agreement," thus the Bible reveals God's covenant or promises to His people. The following are a few Old Testament promises about the Christ, the Son of God, and the New Testament fulfillments by Jesus. Fulfilled prophecy helps verify the fact that Jesus is the Christ.

Topic	Prophecy	Fulfillment
Place of birth	"But you, Bethlehem Ephrathah, though you are small among the clans of Judah, out of you will come for me one who will be ruler over Israel, whose origins are from of old, from ancient times." (Micah 5:2) 700 b.c.	"Jesus was born in Bethlehem in Judea." (Matthew 2:1)
Born of a virgin	"Therefore the Lord himself will give you a sign: The virgin will be with child and will give birth to a son, and will call him Immanuel." (Isaiah 7:14) 700 b.c.	"His mother Mary was pledged to be married to Joseph, but before they came together, she was found to be with child through the Holy Spirit." (Matthew 1:18)

His triumphal entry	"Rejoice greatly, O Daughter of Zion! Shout, Daughter of Jerusalem! See, your king comes to you, righteous and having salvation, gentle and riding on a donkey, on a colt, the foal of a donkey." (Zechariah 9:9) 500 b.c.	"They took palm branches and went out to meet him, shouting, 'Hosanna! Blessed is he who comes in the name of the Lord! Blessed is the King of Israel!' Jesus found a young donkey and sat upon it." (John 12:13-14)
Betrayed by a friend	"Even my close friend, whom I trusted, he who shared my bread, has lifted up his heel against me." (Psalm 41:9) 1000 b.c.	"Then Judas Iscariot, one of the Twelve, went to the chief priests to betray Jesus to them." (Mark 14:10)
His rejection	"He was despised and rejected by men, a man of sorrows, and familiar with suffering. Like one from whom men hide their faces he was despised, and we esteemed him not." (Isaiah 53:3) 700 b.c.	"He came to that which was his own, but his own did not receive him." (John 1:11)
Crucified with sinners	"... he poured out his life unto death, and was numbered with the transgressors." (Isaiah 53:12) 700 b.c.	"Two robbers were crucified with him, one on his right and one on his left." (Matthew 27:38)
Hands and feet pierced	"... they have pierced my hands and my feet." (Psalm 22:16) 1000 b.c.	"Put your finger here; see my hands. Reach out your hand and put it into my side." (John 20:27)

His resurrection	"You will not abandon me to the grave, nor will you let your Holy One see decay." (Psalm 16:10) 1000 b.c.	"You killed the author of life, but God raised him from the dead." (Acts 3:15)
His ascension	"You ascended on high . . ." (Psalm 68:18) 1000 b.c.	"He was taken up before their very eyes, and a cloud hid him from their sight." (Acts 1:9)

6. Jesus believed the Scriptures; in fact, He quoted from over 22 Old Testament books during His time on earth. Match the following verses with the Old Testament people and places Jesus referred to in Matthew alone.

   a. Matt. 5:17, 18   _____ Abraham
   b. Matt. 6:29   _____ Solomon
   c. Matt. 8:4   _____ Sodom and Gomorrah
   d. Matt. 8:11   _____ The law and the prophets
   e. Matt. 10:15   _____ Moses

7. In Luke 24: 13-32, we read about Jesus walking a road with two of His followers. What are they discussing? (verse 19-24)

   _____

   _____

8. What did Jesus explain to them? (verse 25-27)

   _____

   _____

9. What does this say about Jesus' confidence or trust in the Scripture?

_____

_____

10. What kind of bearing should this have on our trust in God's Word?

_____

_____

11. List two things you have discovered for the first time in this study.

_____

_____

_____

12. What more would you like to learn?

_____

_____

_____

_____

Summary

Men throughout history have tried to discredit the Bible and have failed. Some simply call it a good book with some good ideas but have never seriously considered what it says. If the Bible is what it claims to be, it must be taken seriously, as many through the ages can testify. A wise and astute college professor once remarked to his student:

"If you are an intelligent person, you will read the one book that has drawn more attention than any other, *if* you are searching for the truth."

Josh McDowell,
Evidence That Demands A Verdict
(Here's Life Pub. 1979, p. 24)

Scripture Passages

Is The Bible Credible?

2 Timothy 3:14-17

But as for you, continue in what you have learned and have become convinced of, because you know those of whom you learned it, and how from infancy you have known the Holy Scriptures, which are able to make you wise for salvation through faith in Christ Jesus. All Scripture is God-breathed and is useful for teaching, rebuking, correcting, and training in righteousness, so that the man of God may be thoroughly equipped for every good work.

2 Peter 1:19-21

And we have the word of the prophets made more certain, and you will do well to pay attention to it, as to a light shining in a dark place, until the day dawns and the morning star rises in your hearts. Above all, you must understand that no prophecy of Scripture came about by the prophet's own interpretation. For prophecy never had its origin in the will of man, but man spoke from God as they were carried along by the Holy Spirit.

Matthew 5:17-18

Do not think that I have come to abolish the Law or the Prophets; I have not come to abolish them but to fulfill them. I tell you the truth, until heaven and earth disappear, not the smallest letter, not the least stroke of a pen, will by any means disappear from the Law until everything is accomplished.

Matthew 6:29

Yet I tell you that not even Solomon in all his splendor was dressed like one of these.

Matthew 8:4

Then Jesus said to him, "See that you don't tell anyone. But go, show yourself to the priest and offer the gift Moses commanded, as a testimony to them."

Matthew 8:11

"I say to you that many will come from the east and the west, and will take their places at the feast with Abraham, Isaac, and Jacob in the kingdom of heaven."

Matthew 10:15

"I will tell you the truth, it will be more bearable for Sodom and Gomorrah on that day of judgement than for that town."

Luke 24:13-32

Now that same day two of them were going to a village called Emmaus, about seven miles from Jerusalem. They were talking with each other about everything that had happened. As they talked and discussed these things with each other, Jesus himself came up and walked along with them; but they were kept from recognizing him.

He asked them, "What are you discussing together as you walk along?"

They stood still, their faces downcast. One of them, named Cleopas, asked him, "Are you only a visitor to Jerusalem and do not know the things that have happened there in these days?"

"What things?" he asked.

"About Jesus of Nazareth," they replied. "He was a prophet, powerful in word and deed before God and all the people. The chief priests and our rulers handed him over to be sentenced to death, and they crucified him; but we had hoped that he was the one who was going to redeem Israel.

And what is more, it is the third day since all this took place. In addition, some of our women amazed us. They went to the tomb early this morning but didn't find his body. They came and told us that they had seen a vision of angels, who said he was alive. Then some of our companions went to the tomb and found it just as the women had said, but him they did not see."

He said to them, "How foolish you are, and how slow of heart to believe all that the prophets have spoken! Did not the Christ have to suffer these things and then enter his glory?" And beginning with Moses and all the Prophets, he explained to them what was said in all the Scriptures concerning himself.

As they approached the village to which they were going, Jesus acted as if he were going farther. But they urged him strongly, "Stay with us, for it is nearly evening; the day is almost over." So he went in to stay with them.

When he was at the table with them, he took bread, gave thanks, broke it and began to give it to them. Then their eyes were opened and they recognized him, and he disappeared from their sight. They asked each other, "Were not our hearts burning within us while he talked with us on the road and opened the Scriptures to us?"

2

Who Is Jesus Christ?

Jesus once asked his followers, "Who do people say I am?" They replied with a few of the opinions the public had of him at that time. Then Jesus said, "But what about you? Who do you say I am?" (Matthew 16:15).

That question was important then—and it's just as important today. The answer is the foundation for true life.

Jesus Christ is God

1. The Old Testament prophet Isaiah foretold much about a future great servant of God, and his words were fulfilled hundreds of years later by Jesus Christ. What did Isaiah say in Isaiah 9:6 about the titles Christ would have?

_____

_____

_____

_____

_____

_____

_____

2. How did Peter answer Jesus' question in Matthew 16:15-16?

_____

_____

3. Read the account of Jesus walking on the water in Matthew 14:22-33. After his disciples saw this, what did they do? (verse 33)

_____

_____

4. What did Jesus claim about himself in Matthew 28:18?

_____

_____

5. How did Jesus demonstrate his power in Mark 1:40-42?

_____

_____

_____

6. What power does Jesus claim to have in John 5:21?

_____

According to what Jesus said in John 5:40, why do some people not experience what Jesus has to offer?

_____

7. In John 5:22-23, what attitude toward the Son of God did Jesus teach that we should have?

_____

_____

8. Read in John 10:22-33 about a dramatic confrontation Jesus had with some Jews. How did Jesus identify himself with God the Father? (verse 30)

_____

Why did the Jews who heard him speak these words prepare to stone Jesus? (verse 33)

_____

9. Read in John 20:24-28 about the doubts the disciple Thomas had about Jesus Christ's resurrection. What did Thomas say when Jesus later appeared to him? (verse 28)

_____

10. Are you convinced Jesus Christ is God? If so, why?

_____

_____

_____

_____

_____

Jesus Christ's Humanity

11. How is Jesus shown to be human in these verses?

John 4:6 _____

John 11:35 _____

John 19:28 _____

12. According to Hebrews 2:14, why did Jesus come to the earth to live as a human being and to die?

_____

_____

_____

13. Read Hebrews 4:14-15. According to verse 15, how was Jesus like all other people?

_____

_____

_____

_____

_____

How was he different?

_____

_____

_____

_____

_____

_____

_____

_____

Scripture Passages

Who Is Jesus Christ?

Isaiah 9:6

For unto us a child is born,
to us a son is given,
and the government will be on his shoulders.
And he will be called Wonderful Counselor,
Mighty God, Everlasting Father, Prince of Peace.

Matthew 16:15-16

"But what about you?" he asked.
"Who do you say I am?" Simon Peter answered, "You are the Christ, the Son of the living God."

Matthew 14:22-33

Immediately Jesus made the disciples get into the boat and go on ahead of him to the other side, while he dismissed the crowd.

After he had dismissed them, he went up on a mountainside by himself to pray. When evening came, he was there alone, but the boat was already a considerable distance from land, buffeted by the waves because the wind was against it.

During the fourth watch of the night Jesus went out to them, walking on the lake. When the disciples saw him walking on the lake, they were terrified. "It's a ghost," they said, and cried out in fear.

But Jesus immediately said to them: "Take courage! It is I. Don't be afraid."

"Lord, if it's you," Peter replied, "tell me to come to you on the water."

"Come," he said.

Then Peter got down out of the boat, walked on the water and came toward Jesus.

But when he saw the wind, he was afraid and, beginning to sink, cried out, "Lord, save me!"

Immediately Jesus reached out his hand and caught him. "You of little faith," he said, "why did you doubt?"

And when they climbed into the boat, the wind died down. Then those who were in the boat worshiped him, saying, "Truly you are the Son of God."

Matthew 28:18
Then Jesus came to them and said, "All authority in heaven and on earth has been given to me."

Mark 1:40-42
A man with leprosy came to him and begged him on his knees, "If you are willing, you can make me clean."

Filled with compassion, Jesus reached out his hand and touched the man. "I am willing," he said. "Be clean!" Immediately the leprosy left him and he was cured.

John 5:21
"For just as the Father raises the dead and gives them life, even so the Son gives life to whom he is pleased to give it."

John 5:40
"You refuse to come to me to have life."

John 5:22-23
Moreover, the Father judges no one, but has entrusted all judgment to the Son, that all may honor the Son just as they honor the Father. He who does not honor the Son does not honor the Father, who sent him.

John 10:22-33

Then came the Feast of Dedication at Jerusalem. It was winter, and Jesus was in the temple area walking in Solomon's Colonnade. The Jews gathered around him, saying, "How long will you keep us in suspense? If you are the Christ, tell us plainly."

Jesus answered, "I did tell you, but you do not believe. The miracles I do in my Father's name speak for me, but you do not believe because you are not my sheep. My sheep listen to my voice; I know them, and they follow me. I give them eternal life, and they shall never perish; no one can snatch them out of my hand. My Father, who has given them to me, is greater than all; no one can snatch them out of my Father's hand. I and the Father are one."

Again the Jews picked up stones to stone him, but Jesus said to them, "I have shown you many great miracles from the Father. For which of these do you stone me?"

"We are not stoning you for any of these," replied the Jews, "but for blasphemy, because you, a mere man, claim to be God."

John 20:24-28

Now Thomas (called Didymus), one of the Twelve, was not with the disciples when Jesus came. So the other disciples told him, "We have seen the Lord!"

But he said to them, "Unless I see the nail marks in his hands and put my finger where the nails were, and put my hand into his side, I will not believe it."

A week later his disciples were in the house again, and Thomas was with them. Though the doors were locked, Jesus came and stood among them and said, "Peace be with you!" Then he said to Thomas, "Put your finger here; see my hands. Reach out your hand and put it into my side. Stop doubting and believe."

Thomas said to him, "My Lord and my God!"

John 4:6
Jacob's well was there, and Jesus, tired as he was from the journey, sat down by the well. It was about the sixth hour.

John 11:35
Jesus wept.

John 19:28
Later, knowing that all was now completed, and so that the Scripture would be fulfilled, Jesus said, "I am thirsty."

Hebrews 2:14
Since the children have flesh and blood, he too shared in their humanity so that by his death he might destroy him who holds the power of death-that is, the devil.

Hebrews 4:14-15
Therefore, since we have a great high priest who has gone through the heavens, Jesus the Son of God, let us hold firmly to the faith we profess. For we do not have a high priest who is unable to sympathize with our weaknesses, but we have one who has been tempted in every way, just as we are-yet was without sin.

3

What Did Christ Jesus Do?

Jesus healed the sick, raised the dead, fed the hungry multitudes, and was friend to social outcasts and sinners. He spoke words of wisdom and power which astounded his hearers. He lived a sinless life, but was put to death as a common criminal.

But his story doesn't end there. His death, his resurrection, and his ascension into heaven mark the most amazing aspects of his life on earth.

His Death

1. When an angel told Joseph about the coming birth of Jesus (Matthew 1:21), for what purpose did he say Jesus was coming into the world?

_____

_____

_____

2. Read Matthew 16:21. To whom did Jesus talk about his coming suffering, death, and resurrection?

_____

3. According to Matthew 27:26, what kind of death did the Roman governor Pilate sentence Jesus to?

_____

4. What kind of men were executed with Jesus? (Matthew 27:38)

_____

5. According to Romans 5:8, what did the death of Jesus prove about God?

_____

6. Read carefully the prophecy in Isaiah 53:5-6. Why did Jesus Christ suffer?

_____

How is man's sinful attitude described?

_____

_____

Who put the punishment for our sins on Christ?

_____

7. Read 1 Peter 2:24. For what purpose did Christ bear our sins?

_____

_____

8. Read Jesus' words in John 10:17-18. Check one of the following statements which is the best summary of these verses:

□ Jesus went to his death voluntarily, and God loved him for this.

□ Jesus was forced to a premature death by the actions of his enemies.

□ Jesus did not resist his suffering and death because he knew he was powerless to avoid it.

His Resurrection

9. Read John 2:18-22. What did Jesus say would happen to him after he was killed?

_____

10. In Peter's speech near the temple recorded in Acts 3, what did he proclaim in verse 15?

_____

11. According to Acts 4:33, in what manner did the apostles talk about the resurrection of Jesus Christ?

_____

12. Read Romans 1:4. What did the resurrection demonstrate about Christ?

_____

_____

_____

13. According to Paul's words in 1 Corinthians 15: 3-8, what people saw Jesus Christ after his resurrection?

_____

_____

_____

14. According to 1 Corinthians 15:17, why is Christ's resurrection so important for each of us?

_____

_____

_____

_____

_____

His Ascension

15. Read Acts 1:9-11. Where did Jesus ascend to?

_____

16. In John 14:1-2, for what reason did Jesus tell his disciples he was going to heaven?

_____

17. In John 14:3, what else did he promise?

_____

_____

18. Read Paul's statement of prayer in Ephesians 1:18-23. Over how much does Christ now rule? (verse 21-22)

_____

_____

19. Review the questions and your answers in this chapter. Have you learned something that is especially important to you? If so, write it down here, and explain how it can help you:

_____

_____

_____

_____

_____

_____

_____

_____

_____

_____

_____

Scripture Passages

What Did Christ Jesus Do?

Matthew 1:21

> She will give birth to a son, and
> you are to give him the name Jesus,
> because he will save his people from
> their sins.

Matthew 16:21

> From that time on Jesus began to
> explain to his disciples that he must go to Jerusalem and
> suffer many things at the hands of the elders, chief priests
> and teachers of the law, and that he must be killed and on the
> third day be raised to life.

Matthew 27:26

> Then he released Barabbas to them. But he had Jesus
> flogged, and handed him over to be crucified.

Matthew 27:38

> Two robbers were crucified with him, one on his right and
> one on his left.

Romans 5:8

> But God demonstrates his own love for us in this: While we
> were still sinners, Christ died for us.

Isaiah 53:5-6

> But he was pierced for our transgressions, he was crushed
> for our iniquities; the punishment that brought us peace was

upon him, and by his wounds we are healed. We all, like sheep, have gone astray, each of us has turned to his own way; and the LORD has laid on him the iniquity of us all.

1 Peter 2:24

He himself bore our sins in his body on the tree, so that we might die to sins and live for righteousness; by his wounds you have been healed.

John 10:17-18

The reason my Father loves me is that I lay down my life—only to take it up again. No one takes it from me, but I lay it down of my own accord. I have authority to lay it down and authority to take it up again. This command I received from my Father.

John 2:18-22

Then the Jews demanded of him, "What miraculous sign can you show us to prove your authority to do all this?"

Jesus answered them, "Destroy this temple, and I will raise it again in three days."

The Jews replied, "It has taken forty-six years to build this temple, and you are going to raise it in three days?" But the temple he had spoken of was his body. After he was raised from the dead, his disciples recalled what he had said. Then they believed the Scripture and the words that Jesus had spoken.

Acts 3:15

"You killed the author of life, but God raised him from the dead. We are witnesses of this."

Acts 4:33

With great power the apostles continued to testify to the resurrection of the Lord Jesus, and much grace was with them all.

Romans 1:4

...and who through the Spirit of holiness was declared with power to be the Son of God by his resurrection from the dead: Jesus Christ our Lord.

I Corinthians 15:3-8

For what I received I passed on to you as of first importance: that Christ died for our sins according to the Scriptures, that he was buried, that he was raised on the third day according to the Scriptures, and that he appeared to Peter, and then to the Twelve. After that, he appeared to more than five hundred of the brothers at the same time, most of whom are still living, though some have fallen asleep. Then he appeared to James, then to all the apostles, and last of all he appeared to me also, as to one abnormally born.

I Corinthians 15:17

And if Christ has not been raised, your faith is futile; you are still in your sins.

Acts 1:9-11

After he said this, he was taken up before their very eyes, and a cloud hid him from their sight. They were looking intently up into the sky as he was going, when suddenly two men dressed in white stood beside them.

"Men of Galilee," they said, "why do you stand here looking into the sky? This same Jesus, who has been taken from you into heaven, will come back in the same way you have seen him go into heaven."

John 14:1-2

"Do not let your hearts be troubled. Trust in God; trust also in me. In my Father's house are many rooms; if it were not so, I would have told you. I am going there to prepare a place for you.

John 14:3

And if I go and prepare a place for you, I will come back and take you to be with me that you also may be where I am.

Ephesians 1:18-23

I pray also that the eyes of your heart may be enlightened in order that you may know the hope to which he has called you, the riches of his glorious inheritance in the saints, and his incomparably great power for us who believe. That power is like the working of his mighty strength, which he exerted in Christ when he raised him from the dead and seated him at his right hand in the heavenly realms, far above all rule and authority, power and dominion, and every title that can be given, not only in the present age but also in the one to come. And God placed all things under his feet and appointed him to be head over everything for the church, which is his body, the fullness of him who fills everything in every way.

4

How Can We Have Eternal Life?

In every age of history men seek to know the secret of life after death. All of us have only a short period of time on earth, and then we must face eternity.

What does it mean to have eternal life, and how do we get it? The Bible gives us the answers.

The Source of Eternal Life

1. Read John 3:36. What people have eternal life?

_____

What happens to everyone else?

_____

_____

2. In John 14:6, what did Jesus claim about the way in which people can reach God?

_____

3. How did Jesus define eternal life in John 17:3?

_____

_____

4. In Peter's speech in Acts 4: 10-12, what did he say about the source of salvation?

_____

_____

5. What condition affecting all mankind is stated in Romans 3:23?

_____

_____

6. Read Romans 6:23. What results from sin?

_____

Where does eternal life come from?

_____

_____

How Do We Receive Eternal Life?

7. According to John 1:12, what response to Christ must we have in order to become God's children?

_____

8. Read John 11:25. What does Jesus promise?

_____

_____

9. In Acts 10:43, what did the prophets say we receive when we believe in Christ?

_____

_____

10. Read carefully I John 5:11-12. If someone has Christ, what else does he have?

_____

Can he have this without having Christ?

_____

11. According to Ephesians 2:8-9, do our own accomplishments which we achieve in life have anything to do with our being saved? Why or Why not?

_____

Can We Know We Have Eternal Life?

12. When Jesus promised eternal life to those who hear and believe him in John 5:24, with what phrase did he begin his promise?

_____

13. According to Romans 8:35-39, what can cut us off from Christ's love?

_____

14. Read 2 Thessalonians 3:3. What will God do for us?

_____

_____

15. Read 1 John 5:13. What is it that we know?

_____

_____

A Summary Verse

16. Read John 3:16. Who did God love?

_____

What did God's love cause him to do?

_____

What happens to those who believe in his Son?

_____

_____

17. Do you know that you have eternal life? Why or why not?

_____

_____

_____

_____

_____

Scripture Passages

How Can We Have Eternal Life?

John 3:36

> Whoever believes in the Son has eternal life, but whoever rejects the Son will not see life, for God's wrath remains on him.

John 14:6

> Jesus answered, "I am the way and the truth and the life. No one comes to the Father except through me."

John 17:3

> "Now this is eternal life: that they may know you, the only true God, and Jesus Christ, whom you have sent."

Acts 4:10-12

> Then know this, you and all the people of Israel: It is by the name of Jesus Christ of Nazareth, whom you crucified but whom God raised from the dead, that this man stands before you healed. He is "the stone you builders rejected, which has become the capstone." Salvation is found in no one else, for there is no other name under heaven given to men by which we must be saved.

Romans 3:23

> For all have sinned and fall short of the glory of God.

Romans 6:23

> For the wages of sin is death, but the gift of God is eternal life in Christ Jesus our Lord.

John 1:12

> Yet to all who are received him, to those who believed in his name, he gave the right to become children of God.

John 11:25

Jesus said to her, "I am the resurrection and the life. He who believes in me will live, even though he dies."

Acts 10:43

All the prophets testify about him that everyone who believes in him receives forgiveness of sins through his name.

I John 5:11-12

And this is the testimony: God has given us eternal life, and this life is in his Son. He who has the Son has life; he who does not have the Son of God does not have life.

Ephesians 2:8-10

For it is by grace you have been saved, through faith—and this not from yourselves, it is the gift of God—not by works, so that no one can boast. For we are God's workmanship, created in Christ Jesus to do good works, which God prepared in advance for us to do.

John 5:24

I tell you the truth, whoever hears my word and believes him who sent me has eternal life and will not be condemned; he has crossed over from death to life.

Romans 8:35-39

Who shall separate us from the love of Christ? Shall trouble or hardship or persecution or famine or nakedness or danger or sword? As it is written, "For your sake we face death all day long; we are considered as sheep to be slaughtered." No, in all these things we are more than conquerors through him who loved us. For I am convinced that neither death nor life, neither angels nor demons, neither the present nor the future, nor any powers, neither height nor depth, nor anything else in all creation, will be able to separate us from the love of God that is in Christ Jesus our Lord.

2 Thessalonians 3:3

But the Lord is faithful, and he will strengthen and protect you from the evil one.

I John 5:13

I write these things to you who believe in the name of the Son of God so that you may know that you have eternal life.

John 3:16

For God so loved the world that he gave his one and only Son, that whoever believes in him shall not perish but have eternal life.

Notes:

Notes:

Made in United States
North Haven, CT
29 August 2024

56666073R00026